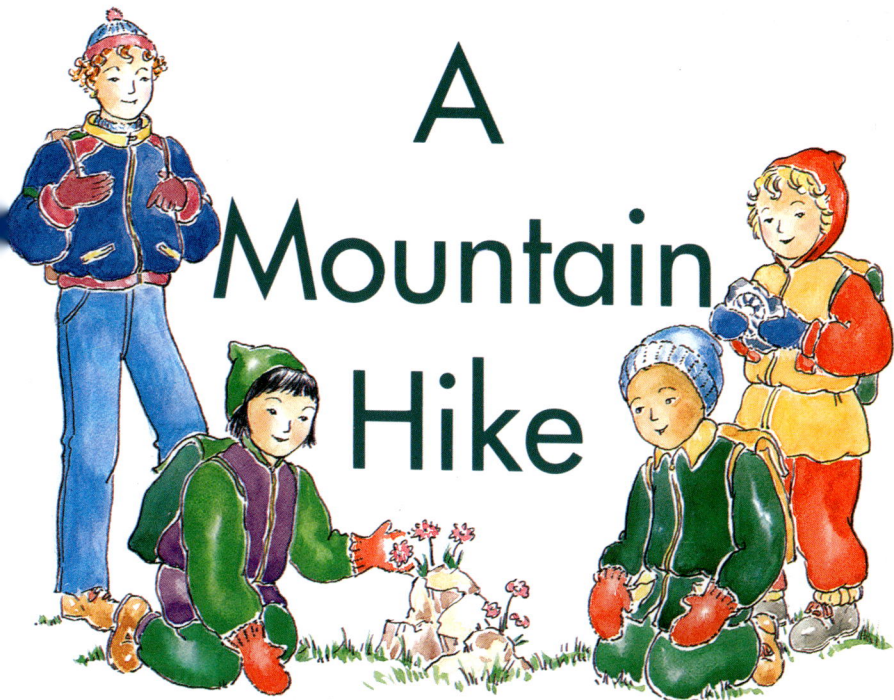

A Mountain Hike

Paul Humphrey and
Alex Ramsay

Illustrated by
Kareen Taylerson

Evans

Mum's taking us hiking up the mountain.

4

We're all wearing our hiking boots.

They have thick rubber soles so that we don't slip on the rocks.

5

What else do we need to take?

We'll need waterproof jackets and warm clothes. It will get colder as we go higher. We must take something to eat and drink as well.

6

I've got some chocolate in my rucksack...

...and I've got a bottle of water.

If we keep to the path and use our map
and compass we won't get lost.

8

You can see where we are on the map. We will use the compass to show us which direction we must walk in.

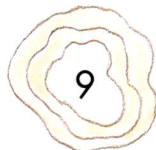

This used to be a quarry where they dug out rock to use for building houses and roads.

Look, this rock has got a shell in it!

That's not a real shell any more, it's a fossil. Millions of years ago it was a living creature. Now all that is left is the shape of the shell in the stone.

12

I've found a lovely, shiny stone.

The shiny bits in the stone are called quartz.

13

Look, there are stepping stones here.
Let's cross the stream.

The water is freezing.
Why is it so cold?

The water is cold because it is
melted snow.

There's always snow at the top of this
mountain. When the sun shines it melts
the snow and the water runs down the
mountain in streams.

There are tiny plants and flowers everywhere.

Those are alpine plants. They grow in sheltered cracks in the rocks where they won't be damaged by the strong winds up here.

16

It is windy,
I'm cold.

It always gets colder as you climb
higher up the mountain. That's why
we all brought extra clothes.
Let's put our sweaters on now.

Why are the trees so small here?

The trees are small because it's harder
for them to grow here. There's only a
very thin layer of soil covering the rocks.

Further up the mountain there won't be any trees at all. If we climb as high as that we will be above the tree-line.

That's a golden eagle. It's diving
on its prey.

It usually eats small animals like rabbits but it has such strong talons that it can even kill foxes.

Look at the river rushing along at the bottom of that deep valley.

It has taken hundreds of years for the water to cut through the rock. The deep valley it has made is called a gorge.

This gorge is about 30 metres
deep. Did you know that the
Grand Canyon in the United States is
1,500 metres deep?

I can see for miles!

The houses down there look tiny.

24

The houses look tiny
because they are so
far below us.
The higher we go the
smaller they will look.

It's so cold up there that the ground is covered in ice and snow all the year round.

In winter the whole mountain will be
covered in snow.

I'm tired
of climbing.

Let's go down now. We must get to the bottom before it gets dark.
Climbing is fun but it's very tiring.

I would like to be a mountaineer when I grow up.

Can you name the things on this page? The answers are at the bottom of the page but don't peep until you have tried yourself.

30